Write Your Best Novel

a workbook to guide you from
concept to publication

Erin Mindes, Stephanie Moore, and Paige Sommer

Welcome!

Hi Friend,

Like you, we're writers. We know at times, the writing process can be a lonely and wandering endeavor. The following pages will help guide, motivate, remind, and inspire your work so that you don't feel alone or lost, whether your word count is 10 or 100,000.

Between the three of us we've attended and helped run over 30 writing conferences. We've created this workbook to keep the writing conference motivation alive. It's meant to be portable, so keep it with you and capture ideas wherever you are.

Your words and stories matter. We're by your side, hoping for your success. Let *Write Your Best Novel* be your guide to make your dreams come true.

Write on!
Erin, Stephanie, and Paige

@writing.friends.society

Table of
Contents

Section 3: Revision Checklist

Section 4: Publishing & Marketing

About the Creators

Glossary of Writing
Abbreviations and Terms

- ARC: Advanced Reader's Copy. Before a book is published, the publisher prints an ARC. It allows them to look for any errors and also gives reviewers a chance to read the book before the release date.
- ASIN: Amazon Standard Identification Number
- EPUB: Electronic Publication
- ISBN: International Standard Book Number is unique code given to all goods for sale.
- MG: Middle Grade (ages 8-12)
- MS or MSS: Manuscript(s)
- NA: New Adult (ages 18-24)
- PB: Picture Book
- POD: Print On Demand is used mainly in self publishing. It's when a book is printed through an online site when someone orders it.
- POV: Point of View
- RWA: Romance Writers of America
- SCBWI: Society of Children's Book Writers and Illustrators
- SF: Science Fiction
- SF/F: Science Fiction and Fantasy
- WIP: Work In Progress
- YA: Young Adult (ages 13-18)

Glossary of Writing
Abbreviations and Terms

- Advance: Publishers will give an author a certain amount of money upfront. The money is an advance against the author's royalties.
- Beta Readers: Readers who critique drafts of a manuscript for the author.
- Character Arc: The character arc is the internal, emotional journey the main character goes on in the course of the novel.
- Manuscript Wish List: This is a list of topics and genres that agents and editors are actively looking to acquire.
- Out of Print: Publishers do print orders, with a certain number of books depending on what they think the demand will be for each novel. If books don't sell well enough after a certain amount of time, the publisher will stop printing them and the book will be considered "out of print".
- Pantser: A person that writes by the "seat of their pants". They discover plot and scenes as they write the first draft of their novel.
- Pitch: A 2-3 sentence hook that describes your manuscript.
- Plotter: A person that outlines and plots out their novel before they begin writing.
- Query: A letter to an agent or editor explaining your story and inviting them to review your full manuscript.
- Royalties: The monetary percentage of book sales the author receives.
- Synopsis: A 1-2 page summary of the events in the novel. Do not hide the ending.

Section 1:
Goals

It's delightful when your imaginations come true, isn't it?

— L.M. Montgomery, *Anne of Green Gables*

Writing Life
Big Picture

You are a writer when you say you are a writer.
Period.

WHAT DOES WRITING SUCCESS LOOK LIKE FOR ME?

WHERE DO I WANT MY WRITING TO BE IN FIVE YEARS?

WHAT CAN I ACCOMPLISH THAT IS IN MY CONTROL?

WHAT STEPS WILL I TAKE TO LEARN MORE AND IMPROVE MY CRAFT?

WHAT WILL I DO TO PRIORITIZE MY WRITING? HOW WILL I MAKE THIS HAPPEN?

Writing Project
Goals

DAILY WORD COUNT GOAL:

DATE I WILL FINISH DRAFTING:

REVISION GOAL DEADLINE:

DATE I WILL SEND TO BETA READERS:

HAVE FINAL EDITS DONE:

START SUBMISSIONS/SELF-PUB DATE:

BEGIN NEXT PROJECT DATE:

MY MOTIVATION:

One word, one sentence, one paragraph, one page:
every effort gets you closer to The End.

Writing Goals

Notes

Word Count
Tracker

<table>
<tr><td>☐ 1500</td><td>☐ 5000</td><td>☐ 8000</td></tr>
<tr><td>☐ 10,000*</td><td>☐ 15,000</td><td>☐ 20,000</td></tr>
<tr><td>☐ 25,000</td><td>☐ 30,000*</td><td>☐ 35,000</td></tr>
<tr><td>☐ 40,000</td><td>☐ 45,000</td><td>☐ 50,000*</td></tr>
<tr><td>☐ 55,000</td><td>☐ 60,000</td><td>☐ 65,000</td></tr>
<tr><td>☐ 70,000</td><td>☐ 75,000*</td><td>☐ 80,000</td></tr>
<tr><td>☐ 85,000</td><td>☐ 90,000</td><td>☐ 100,000</td></tr>
</table>

*The End**

✱ Milestone. Reward yourself!

Daily Word Count
Tracker

YOU CAN DO IT!

Word Count
Tracker

☐ *1500*   ☐ *5000*   ☐ *8000*

☐ *10,000*＊   ☐ *15,000*   ☐ *20,000*

☐ *25,000*   ☐ *30,000*＊   ☐ *35,000*

☐ *40,000*   ☐ *45,000*   ☐ *50,000*＊

☐ *55,000*   ☐ *60,000*   ☐ *65,000*

☐ *70,000*   ☐ *75,000*＊   ☐ *80,000*

☐ *85,000*   ☐ *90,000*   ☐ *100,000*

The End＊

✴ Milestone. Reward yourself!

Daily Word Count
Tracker

YOU CAN DO IT!

Section 2:
The Story

I cannot live without brainwork. What else is there to live for?

— Sir Arthur Conan Doyle, *The Complete Sherlock Holmes*

Get to Know Your
Characters

Characters give stories life.

When you create a character, you come up with their physical features, likes and dislikes, strengths and weaknesses, and everything else that makes them dynamic.

Throughout your novel, your characters will grow and develop as you put them through experiences and decide how they will react. There should be a substantial change in your main character when comparing them to who they were at the beginning to who they become in the end.

The challenges and experiences your characters go through connect them to your readers. They'll keep turning pages because they have to find out what happens. Do they catch the bad guy? Who will they end up with? Do they achieve their dreams?

So before you take your reader on a journey, fill out the following sheets to better understand your characters.

Name:_________________________

Nickname:_______________

Age/Grade:________________

Birthday:__________________

Hair Color:________________

Eye Color:_________________

Skin Color:________________

Species (if applies):________

____
Physical/Mental Disabilities:

____
Birthmarks/Physical Features: ____________________

____
Voice Descriptions: _______________________________

Tics/Involuntary Movements: _____________________

Nervous Habits: __________________________________

Where do they live?	Family	Interests/Hobbies	Musical Talents

Sports/Skills	Job/Career	School	Love Interest

Wants (Internal/External)	Needs (Internal/External)	Fears	Worries

Strengths	Weaknesses	Flaws	Quirks

How are they going to change? (Internally/Externally):

____

____

What motivates them? ____________________________

What are their goals?____________________________

How has their past influenced them? _____________

What would make them suffer?_____________________

What do they need to learn?______________________

Who will help them? _____________________________

Who can/can't they trust?________________________

Who is their nemesis? Or who wants to prevent them from
succeeding? _____________________________________

____

____

Name:_______________________

Nickname:_______________

Age/Grade:_______________

Birthday:_________________

Hair Color:_______________

Eye Color:________________

Skin Color:_______________

Species (if applies):________

____

Physical/Mental Disabilities:

____

Birthmarks/Physical Features: _______________

____

Voice Descriptions: ________________________

Tics/Involuntary Movements: _________________

Nervous Habits: ___________________________

Where do they live?	Family	Interests/Hobbies	Musical Talents

Sports/Skills	Job/Career	School	Love Interest

Wants (Internal/External)	Needs (Internal/External)	Fears	Worries

Strengths	Weaknesses	Flaws	Quirks

How are they going to change? (Internally/Externally):

____

____

What motivates them? ____________________________

What are their goals?____________________________

How has their past influenced them? ______________

What would make them suffer?_____________________

What do they need to learn?_______________________

Who will help them? _____________________________

Who can/can't they trust?_________________________

Who is their nemesis? Or who wants to prevent them from
succeeding? _____________________________________

____

____

Name:_______________________

Nickname:_______________

Age/Grade:________________

Birthday:_________________

Hair Color:_______________

Eye Color:________________

Skin Color:_______________

Species (if applies):________

____
Physical/Mental Disabilities:

____
Birthmarks/Physical Features: _______________

____
Voice Descriptions: _____________________

Tics/Involuntary Movements: ______________

Nervous Habits: ______________________________

Where do they live?	Family	Interests/Hobbies	Musical Talents

Sports/Skills	Job/Career	School	Love Interest

Wants (Internal/External)	Needs (Internal/External)	Fears	Worries

Strengths	Weaknesses	Flaws	Quirks

How are they going to change? (Internally/Externally):

____

____

What motivates them? ___________________________

____

What are their goals?___________________________

____

How has their past influenced them? _____________

____

What would make them suffer?____________________

____

What do they need to learn?______________________

____

Who will help them? _____________________________

____

Who can/can't they trust?_________________________

____

Who is their nemesis? Or who wants to prevent them from
succeeding? ______________________________________

____

____

Name:_______________________

Nickname:_______________________

Age/Grade:_______________________

Birthday:_______________________

Hair Color:_______________________

Eye Color:_______________________

Skin Color:_______________________

Species (if applies):_______________________

____

Physical/Mental Disabilities:

____

Birthmarks/Physical Features: _______________________

____

Voice Descriptions: _______________________

Tics/Involuntary Movements: _______________________

Nervous Habits: _______________________

SKETCH YOUR CHARACTER

Where do they live?	Family	Interests/Hobbies	Musical Talents

Sports/Skills	Job/Career	School	Love Interest

Wants (Internal/External)	Needs (Internal/External)	Fears	Worries

Strengths	Weaknesses	Flaws	Quirks

How are they going to change? (Internally/Externally):

____

____

What motivates them? ____

What are their goals?____

How has their past influenced them? ______________________________

What would make them suffer?____________________________________

What do they need to learn?______________________________________

Who will help them? ____

Who can/can't they trust?____

Who is their nemesis? Or who wants to prevent them from
succeeding? ____

____

____

Name:_____________________

Nickname:_____________________

Age/Grade:_____________________

Birthday:_____________________

Hair Color:_____________________

Eye Color:_____________________

Skin Color:_____________________

Species (if applies):_________

____

Physical/Mental Disabilities:

____

Birthmarks/Physical Features: _________________

____

Voice Descriptions: _________________________

Tics/Involuntary Movements: _________________

Nervous Habits: _____________________________

Where do they live?	Family	Interests/Hobbies	Musical Talents

Sports/Skills	Job/Career	School	Love Interest

Wants (Internal/External)	Needs (Internal/External)	Fears	Worries

Strengths	Weaknesses	Flaws	Quirks

How are they going to change? (Internally/Externally):

____

____

What motivates them? ___________________________________

____

What are their goals?___________________________________

____

How has their past influenced them? _____________________

____

What would make them suffer?___________________________

____

What do they need to learn?_____________________________

____

Who will help them? ____________________________________

____

Who can/can't they trust?_______________________________

____

Who is their nemesis? Or who wants to prevent them from
succeeding? ____

____

____

Name:_______________________

Nickname:_______________

Age/Grade:_______________

Birthday:_______________

Hair Color:_______________

Eye Color:_______________

Skin Color:_______________

Species (if applies):_________

____

Physical/Mental Disabilities:

____

Birthmarks/Physical Features: _____________________

____

Voice Descriptions: _______________________________

Tics/Involuntary Movements: ______________________

Nervous Habits: _________________________________

Where do they live?	Family	Interests/Hobbies	Musical Talents

Sports/Skills	Job/Career	School	Love Interest

Wants (Internal/External)	Needs (Internal/External)	Fears	Worries

Strengths	Weaknesses	Flaws	Quirks

How are they going to change? (Internally/Externally):

____

What motivates them? _____________________________

What are their goals?_____________________________

How has their past influenced them? ______________

What would make them suffer?_____________________

What do they need to learn?_______________________

Who will help them? ______________________________

Who can/can't they trust?_________________________

Who is their nemesis? Or who wants to prevent them from
succeeding? _______________________________________

____

____

Name:_______________________

Nickname:_______________________

Age/Grade:_______________________

Birthday:_______________________

Hair Color:_______________________

Eye Color:_______________________

Skin Color:_______________________

Species (if applies):_______________________

Physical/Mental Disabilities:_______________________

Birthmarks/Physical Features: _______________________

Voice Descriptions: _______________________

Tics/Involuntary Movements: _______________________

Nervous Habits: _______________________

Where do they live?	Family	Interests/Hobbies	Musical Talents

Sports/Skills	Job/Career	School	Love Interest

Wants (Internal/External)	Needs (Internal/External)	Fears	Worries

Strengths	Weaknesses	Flaws	Quirks

How are they going to change? (Internally/Externally):

____

What motivates them? _______________________________

What are their goals?_______________________________

How has their past influenced them? ________________

What would make them suffer?_______________________

What do they need to learn?_________________________

Who will help them? _______________________________

Who can/can't they trust?___________________________

Who is their nemesis? Or who wants to prevent them from
succeeding? ______________________________________

____

____

Name:_______________________

Nickname:_______________________

Age/Grade:_______________________

Birthday:_______________________

Hair Color:_______________________

Eye Color:_______________________

Skin Color:_______________________

Species (if applies):_______________________

Physical/Mental Disabilities:

____

Birthmarks/Physical Features: _______________________

____

Voice Descriptions: _______________________

Tics/Involuntary Movements: _______________________

Nervous Habits: _______________________

Where do they live?	Family	Interests/Hobbies	Musical Talents

Sports/Skills	Job/Career	School	Love Interest

<table>
<tr><td>Wants
(Internal/External)</td><td>Needs
(Internal/External)</td><td>Fears</td><td>Worries</td></tr>
<tr><td></td><td></td><td></td><td></td></tr>
</table>

<table>
<tr><td>Strengths</td><td>Weaknesses</td><td>Flaws</td><td>Quirks</td></tr>
<tr><td></td><td></td><td></td><td></td></tr>
</table>

How are they going to change? (Internally/Externally):

____

____

What motivates them? _____________________________

What are their goals?_____________________________

How has their past influenced them? ______________

What would make them suffer?______________________

What do they need to learn?_______________________

Who will help them? ______________________________

Who can/can't they trust?_________________________

Who is their nemesis? Or who wants to prevent them from
succeeding? ______________________________________

____

____

Name:_______________________

Nickname:______________

Age/Grade:________________

Birthday:__________________

Hair Color:_______________

Eye Color:________________

Skin Color:_______________

Species (if applies):________

____

Physical/Mental Disabilities:

____

Birthmarks/Physical Features: _________________

____

Voice Descriptions: ________________________

Tics/Involuntary Movements: _________________

Nervous Habits: ___________________________

Where do they live?	Family	Interests/Hobbies	Musical Talents

Sports/Skills	Job/Career	School	Love Interest

Wants (Internal/External)	Needs (Internal/External)	Fears	Worries

Strengths	Weaknesses	Flaws	Quirks

How are they going to change? (Internally/Externally):

____

____

What motivates them? ____________________________

What are their goals?____________________________

How has their past influenced them? _____________

What would make them suffer?_____________________

What do they need to learn?______________________

Who will help them? _____________________________

Who can/can't they trust?________________________

Who is their nemesis? Or who wants to prevent them from
succeeding? _____________________________________

____

____

Name:_______________________

Nickname:_______________________

Age/Grade:_______________________

Birthday:_______________________

Hair Color:_______________________

Eye Color:_______________________

Skin Color:_______________________

Species (if applies):_______________________

Physical/Mental Disabilities:
____

Birthmarks/Physical Features: _______________________

Voice Descriptions: _______________________

Tics/Involuntary Movements: _______________________

Nervous Habits: _______________________

SKETCH YOUR CHARACTER

Where do they live?	Family	Interests/Hobbies	Musical Talents

Sports/Skills	Job/Career	School	Love Interest

32

| Wants | Needs | Fears | Worries |
(Internal/External)	(Internal/External)		

Strengths	Weaknesses	Flaws	Quirks

How are they going to change? (Internally/Externally):

____

____

What motivates them? ____

What are their goals?____

How has their past influenced them? ____

What would make them suffer?____

What do they need to learn?____

Who will help them? ____

Who can/can't they trust?____

Who is their nemesis? Or who wants to prevent them from
succeeding? ____

____

____

Name:_________________________

Nickname:_______________

Age/Grade:________________

Birthday:_________________

Hair Color:_______________

Eye Color:________________

Skin Color:_______________

Species (if applies):________

____

Physical/Mental Disabilities:

SKETCH YOUR CHARACTER

____

Birthmarks/Physical Features: _____________________

____

Voice Descriptions: ______________________________

Tics/Involuntary Movements: ______________________

Nervous Habits: __________________________________

Where do they live?	Family	Interests/Hobbies	Musical Talents

Sports/Skills	Job/Career	School	Love Interest

34

Wants (Internal/External)	Needs (Internal/External)	Fears	Worries

Strengths	Weaknesses	Flaws	Quirks

How are they going to change? (Internally/Externally):

____

____

What motivates them? _____________________________

____

What are their goals? _____________________________

____

How has their past influenced them? ________________

____

What would make them suffer? _____________________

____

What do they need to learn? _______________________

____

Who will help them? ______________________________

____

Who can/can't they trust? _________________________

____

Who is their nemesis? Or who wants to prevent them from succeeding? _________________________________

____

____

Character
Spreadsheet

Sometimes you just need a quick look at character specifics to stay consistent throughout your story. Use the list below to inform your thinking on what traits you need to remember about your characters.

Age	Hair Color
Attitude	Hobbies
Backstory	Internal Needs/Wants
Celebrity Look-alike	Language
Core Traits	Main Goal
Dialog Style	Motivation
Dreams	Nickname
Ethnicity	Occupation
External Needs/Wants	Physical Features
Eye Color	Planet
Family Life	Quirks
Favorite Books	Relationship to MC
Favorite Movies	Role or Purpose
Favorite Music	Secrets
Fears	Sex
First Appearance	Skills/Knowledge/Props
Flaws	Values
Full Name	Zodiac Sign
Habits (good/bad)	

Character	Trait 1	Trait 2	Trait 3

Character	Trait 1	Trait 2	Trait 3

Character	Trait 1	Trait 2	Trait 3

Family *Diagram*

For better or worse, all characters have a family. Those relationships play an important role in your main character's journey.

Whether they are siblings, parents, grandparents, extended family or found family, keeping a visual family diagram will help you see or understand their relationships better.

FAMILY CHART INSTRUCTIONS:

1. Write the main character's name in the center oval.
2. Fill in family member's names in the outer ovals.
3. Write their relationships on the lines.

Family
Chart

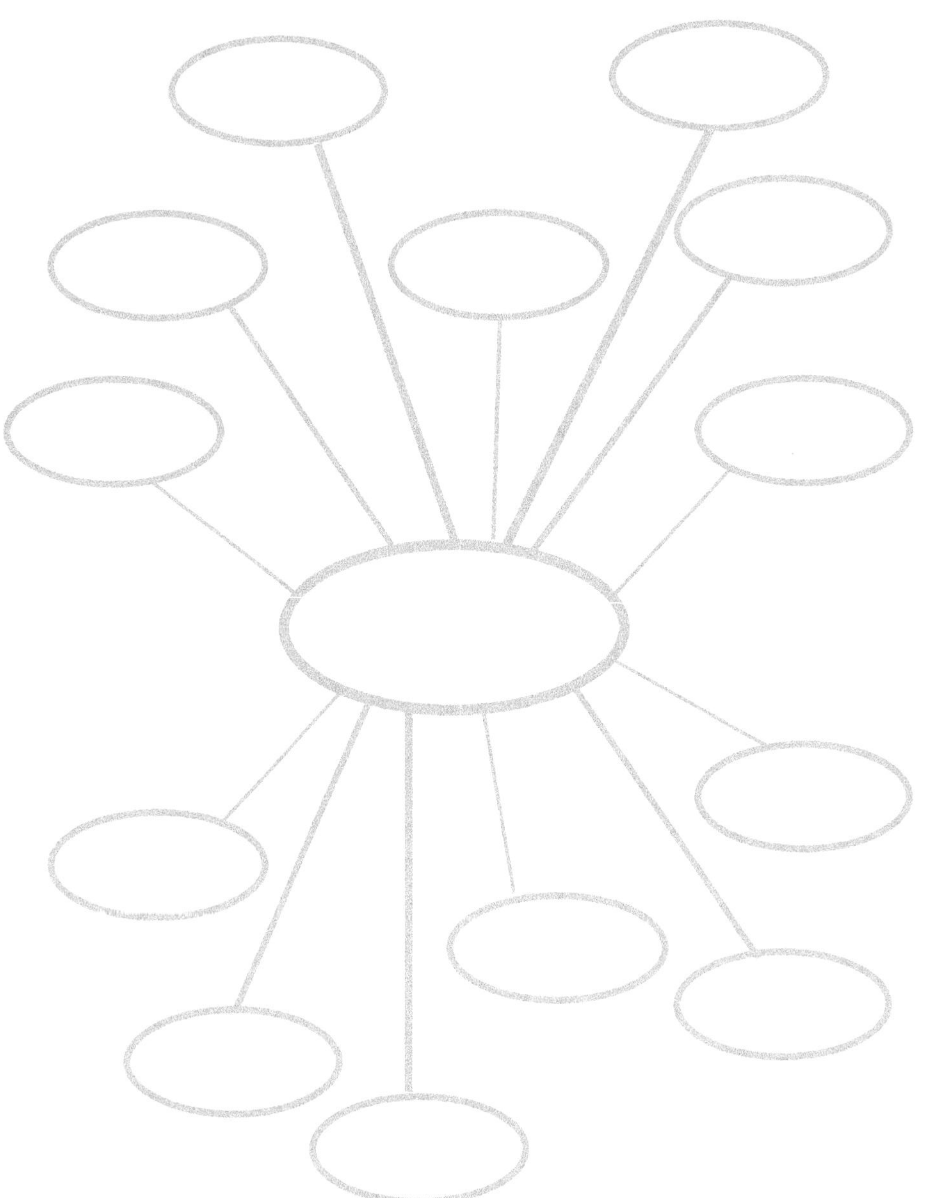

Family *Chart*

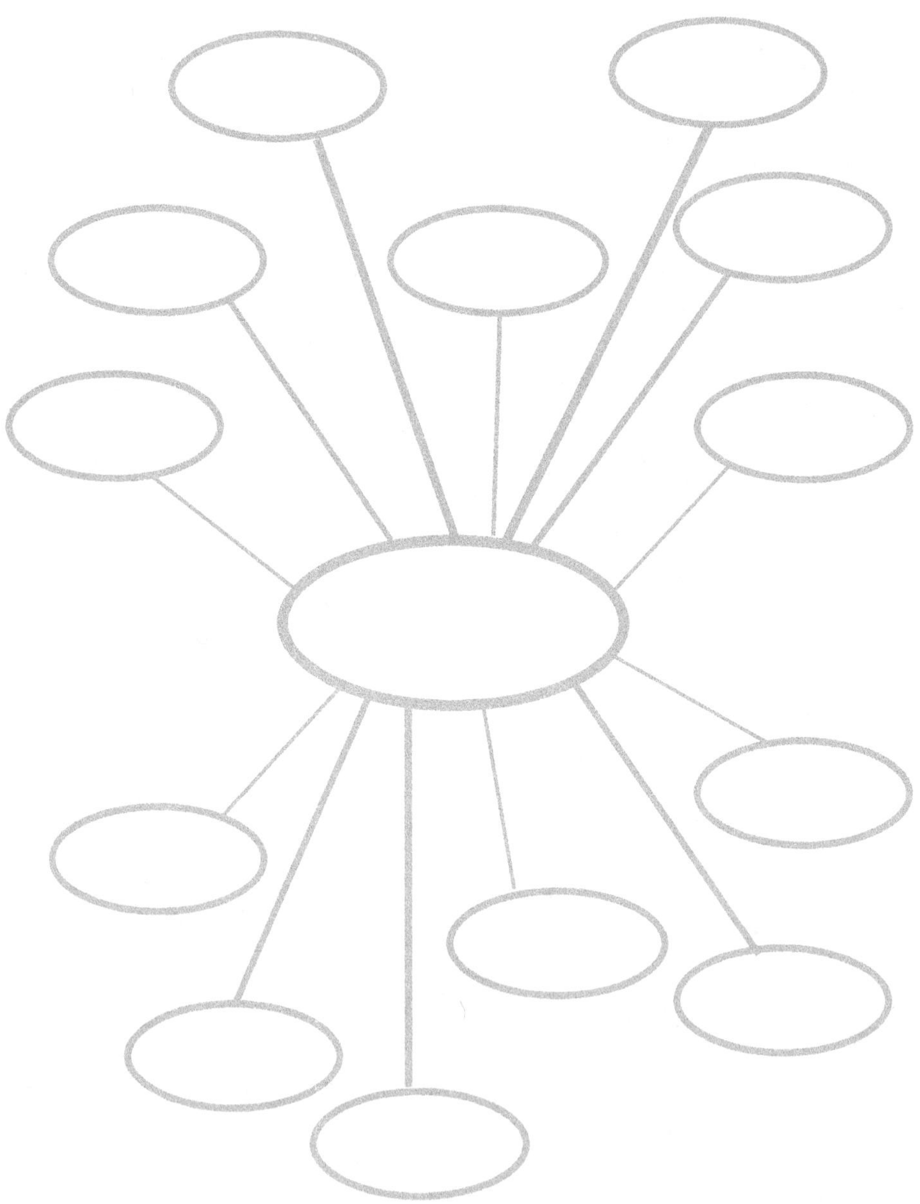

Family Dynamics
Notes

What makes this family unique and
what are their quirks?

Character
Relationship Map

Character connections provide more opportunities to deepen the complexity of your story.

1. Make boxes with character names.
2. Draw lines connecting characters.
3. Write their relationships on the lines.

Here is an example:

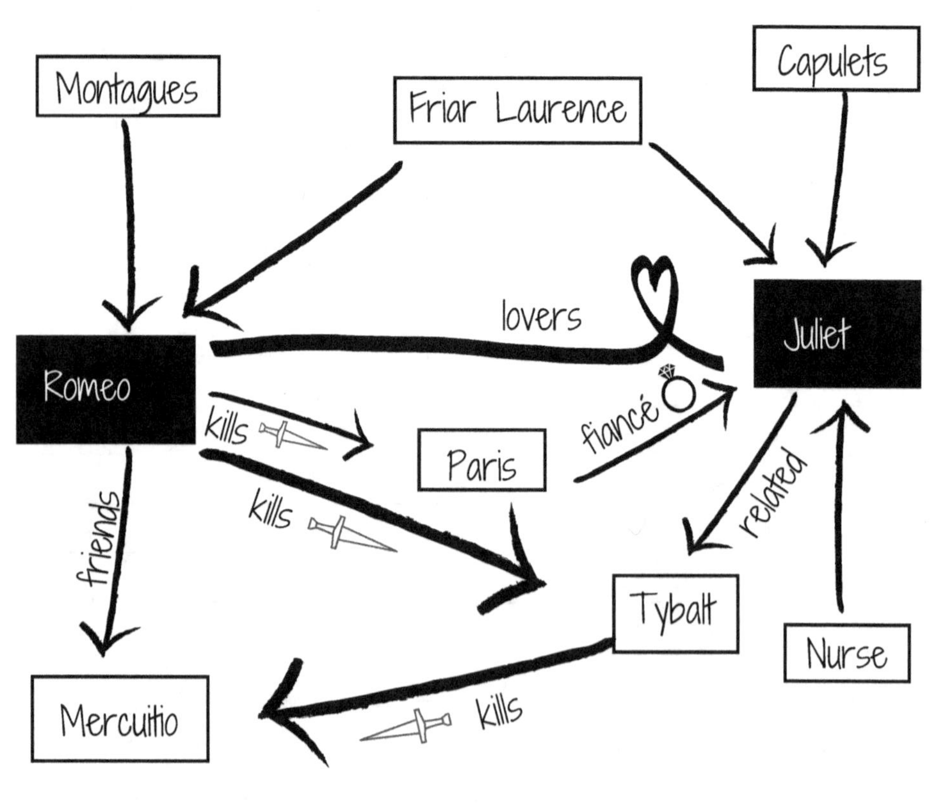

Character
Relationship Map

Character
Relationship Map

Character
Relationship Map

Story
Research

Keep track of important research information here.

Topic:

Reference Location:

Discovery:

Topic:

Reference Location:

Discovery:

Topic:

Reference Location:

Discovery:

Topic:

Reference Location:

Discovery:

Topic:

Reference Location:

Discovery:

Topic:

Reference Location:

Discovery:

Topic:

Reference Location:

Discovery:

Topic:

Reference Location:

Discovery:

Topic:

Reference Location:

Discovery:

Topic:

Reference Location:

Discovery:

Topic:

Reference Location:

Discovery:

Topic:

Reference Location:

Discovery:

Topic:

Reference Location:

Discovery:

Topic:

Reference Location:

Discovery:

Topic:

Reference Location:

Discovery:

Topic:

Reference Location:

Discovery:

Topic:

Reference Location:

Discovery:

World
Building

No matter your genre or setting, all stories need world building. Create your story's world and keep it consistent.

Information to remember about your world:

____
____
____
____
____
____
____
____
____
____
____
____
____
____
____
____
____
____

World
Building

Make it as real as possible.

What are the basic needs?

How do people get food and water?

What are their modes of transportation?

What materials do they use?

What do they do when someone is sick?

Are there city areas and country areas?

What is the geography?

What kind of leader(s) do they have?

What are their holidays or rituals?

What is important to this world?

World Building
Notes

Magic
System

Information to remember about your magic system:

Magic
System

Make it believable

Who has magic?

How do they get magic?

What is the magic called?

What can it do?

What is used to control the magic?
Certain items? Inner power?

What are the consequences for using magic?

What else is important to the magic system in your world?

What is the relationship between magic and non-magic characters?

Magic System
Notes

Story
Settings

Setting is where your story takes place. Novels contain many scenes and with that many locations. The setting affects how your characters behave and how they will react.

Your setting should be as real to you as your characters. Describe each location to make them come alive for your reader.

PLACE: ____

____

____

____

____

____

____

PLACE: ____

____

____

____

____

____

____

PLACE:

PLACE:

PLACE:

PLACE:

PLACE:

PLACE:

PLACE:

PLACE:

PLACE:

Setting
Exercises

What are some key locations for your main character?
Describe them from their point of view.

PLACE: ____

____

____

____

____

____

____

____

PLACE: ____

____

____

____

____

____

____

____

____

PLACE:

PLACE:

PLACE:

Setting
Sketch Area

You don't have to be an artist to make this page work for you. Your sketches could range from the landscape of your character's world to the inside of their locker. It doesn't have to be perfect, even the smallest detail can make a difference.

Setting
Sketch Area

Setting
Sketch Area

Artist
Information

If your story needs illustration, keep track of
freelance artists you like here.

Artist:

Contact Information:

Why they would be good for this project:

Artist:

Contact Information:

Why they would be good for this project:

Artist:

Contact Information:

Why they would be good for this project:

Title
Ideas

Titles help readers get a feel for your book. Your title should be intriguing and original, convey the genre, and be specific to your story.

Note: Publishers have the final decision on the title of the book.

Working Title

Story Elements or Symbols

Possible Titles

Story
Themes

A story's theme is the main, underlying message.

Major Themes: ideas or messages the author returns to over and over, the most important ideas in the story.

Minor Themes: ideas that show up in your story periodically.

It may be helpful to know what themes you want to incorporate into your story before you begin. Or you may discover them as you write.

Identifying theme is a good exercise before, during, and after you draft.

Here's a list to help you generate theme ideas:

Acceptance	Friendship	Love
Anger	Good vs Evil	Loyalty
Believing in Self	Grief	Peace
Belonging	Growing Up	Perseverance
Cirle of Life	Happiness	Power
Coming of Age	Heroism	Prejudice
Compassion	Honesty	Revenge
Cooperation	Individual	Society
Corruption	Jealousy	Survival
Courage	Judgement	New Things
Death	Loss	War

Here are some questions to help you brainstorm the themes in your story:

Why are you writing this story? What story are you hoping to tell?

____

____

____

____

Which themes are the most interesting and meaningful to you?

____

____

____

____

____

What details in your story best show the major and minor themes?

____

____

____

____

____

____

How do the actions or thoughts of your characters help to illustrate your theme?

____

____

____

____

After brainstorming, what are themes in your story?

Major Themes:

How are these incorporated?

Minor Themes:

How are these incorporated?

Story
Outline

Whether you fill this out before or after you've completed your manuscript, this chart will help you see plot holes, or where setting, character, and conflict need to be expounded. Do this exercise for each draft of your story.

Theme: The underlying message or central idea of the story.

Setting	Characters	Conflict
General location.	The main players of the story.	Main problem.

Inciting Incident	Goal & Motivation	Character Arc
Event that sets the MC on their journey.	What the MC needs and wants.	How the MC grows and changes.

Rising Acting	Climax	Conclusion
Events that lead to the climax.	Highest point of tension.	Conflict and character resolution.

Theme:

| Setting | Characters | Conflict |

| Inciting Incident | Goal & Motivation | Changes in MC |

| Rising Acting | Climax | Conclusion |

Theme:

| Setting | Characters | Conflict |

| Inciting Incident | Goal & Motivation | Changes in MC |

| Rising Acting | Climax | Conclusion |

Theme:

| Setting | Characters | Conflict |

| Inciting Incident | Goal & Motivation | Changes in MC |

| Rising Acting | Climax | Conclusion |

Story
Timeline

Create a timeline for plots, character arcs,
important events, or scenes.

Example: Cinderella

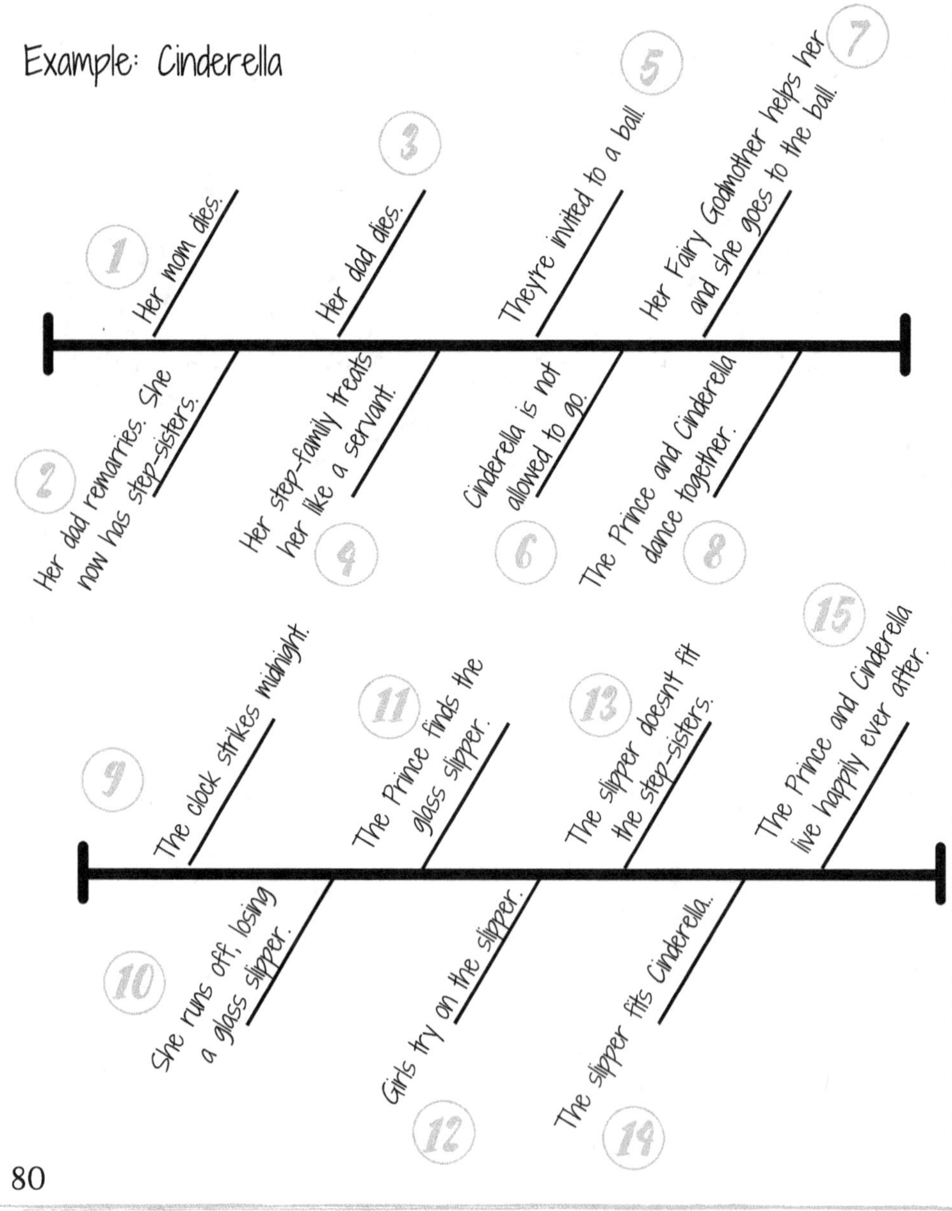

Story
Timeline

Create a timeline for plots, character arcs,
important events, or scenes.

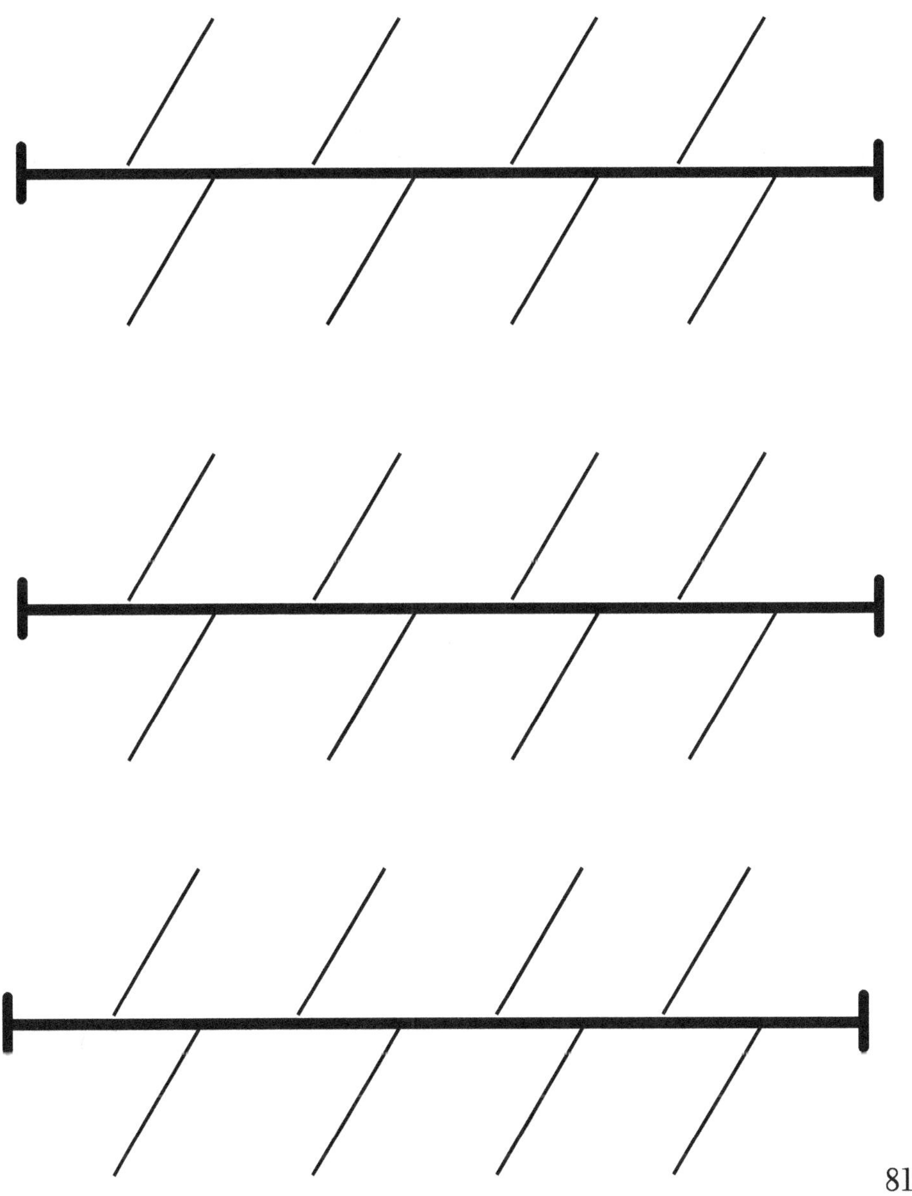

Story
Timeline

Create a timeline for plots, character arcs,
important events, or scenes.

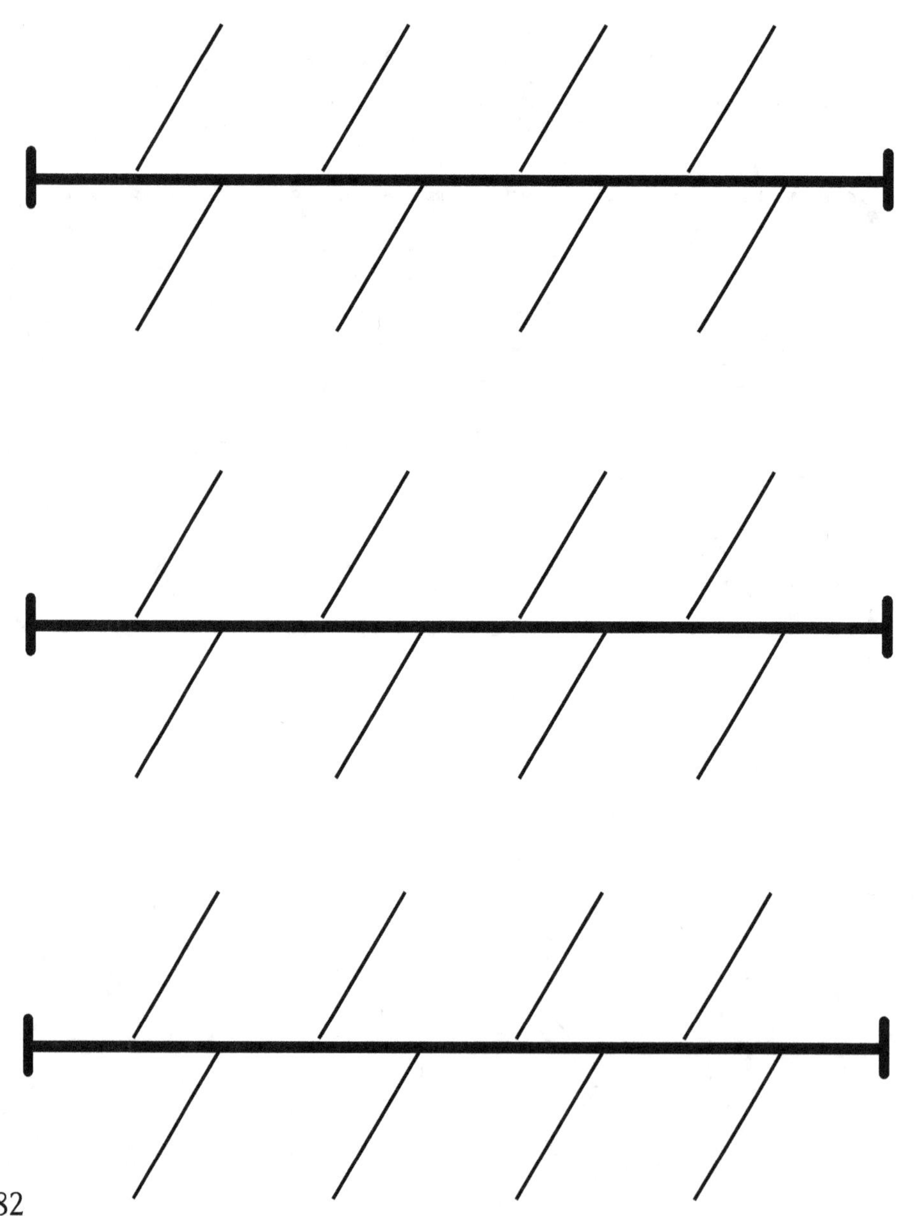

Story
Timeline

Create a timeline for plots, character arcs,
important events, or scenes.

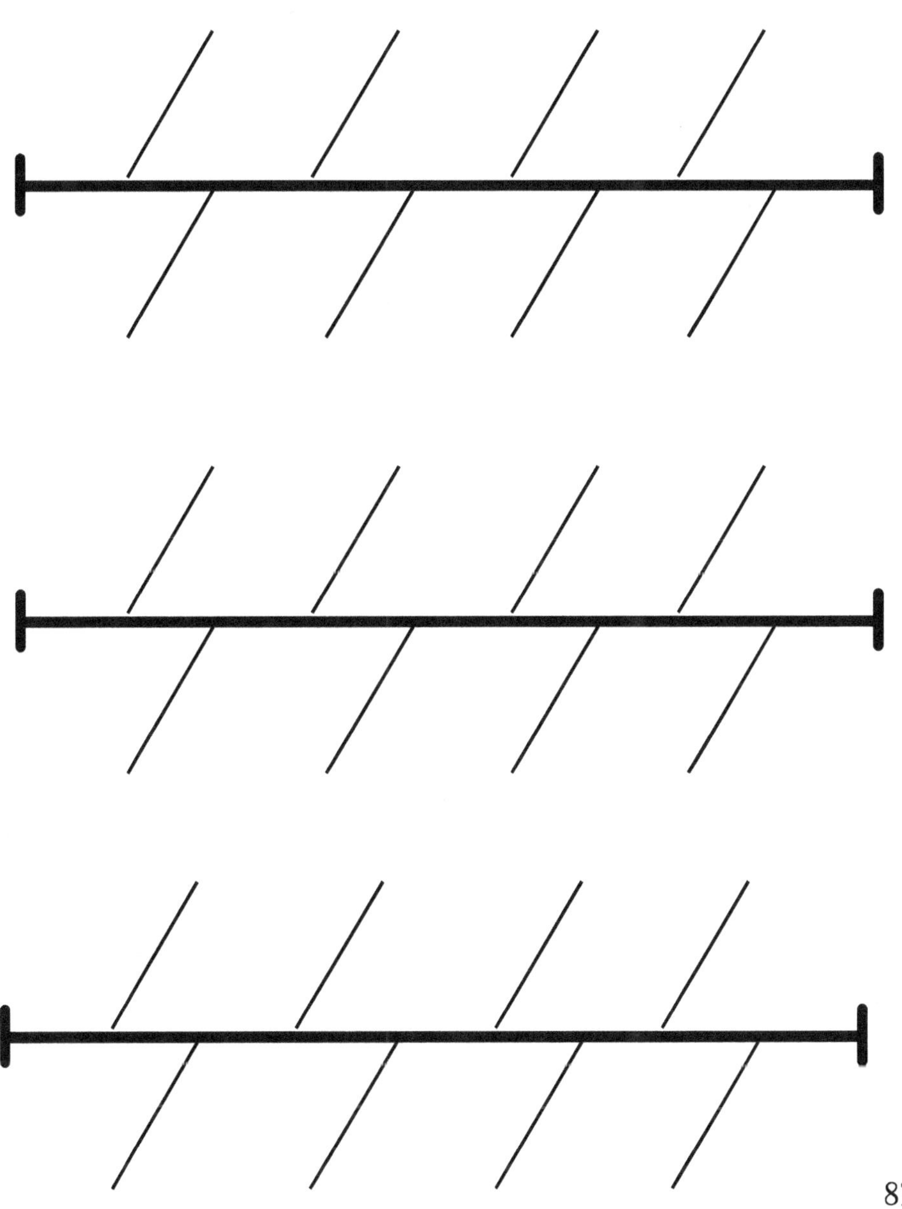

Timeline
Chart

A timeline chart helps keep track of events in your story as they occur in hours, days, weeks, months, or years. Use this chart to keep timing details clear.

Here are some examples:

Romeo and Juliet by William Shakespeare

Act/Ch/Pg	Day	Time	Plot
Act 2	Sunday	Late Evening	Romeo/Juliet Balcony Scene
Act 2	Monday	Early Morning	Romeo goes to Friar

New Moon by Stephenie Meyer

Act/Ch/Pg	Day	Time	Plot
Ch 3	September	Night	Edward leaves Bella brokenhearted
Ch 6	After January	Day	Bella and Jacob hang out

Act/Ch/Pg	Day	Time	Plot

Act/Ch/Pg	Day	Time	Plot

Act/Ch/Pg	Day	Time	Plot

Act/Ch/Pg	Day	Time	Plot

Act/Ch/Pg	Day	Time	Plot
Act/Ch/Pg	Day	Time	Plot

Chapter Titles &
Summaries

You may have to write a synopsis as you prepare to send your work to agents. Keep track along the way or fill in the information after your first draft.

Write a brief summary of each chapter or scene in the order they occur.

______Chapter #/ Chapter Title_______________________________

Brief Summary

______Chapter #/ Chapter Title_______________________________

Brief Summary

_______Chapter #/ Chapter Title_________________________________

Brief Summary

_______Chapter #/ Chapter Title_________________________________

Brief Summary

_______Chapter #/ Chapter Title_________________________________

Brief Summary

______Chapter #/ Chapter Title_____________________________

Brief Summary

______Chapter #/ Chapter Title_____________________________

Brief Summary

______Chapter #/ Chapter Title_____________________________

Brief Summary

_______Chapter #/ Chapter Title_______________________________

Brief Summary

_______Chapter #/ Chapter Title_______________________________

Brief Summary

_______Chapter #/ Chapter Title_______________________________

Brief Summary

_______Chapter #/ Chapter Title________________________________

Brief Summary

_______Chapter #/ Chapter Title________________________________

Brief Summary

_______Chapter #/ Chapter Title________________________________

Brief Summary

______Chapter #/ Chapter Title________________________________

Brief Summary

______Chapter #/ Chapter Title_____________________________

Brief Summary

______Chapter #/ Chapter Title________________________________

Brief Summary

_______Chapter #/ Chapter Title___________________________

Brief Summary

_______Chapter #/ Chapter Title___________________________

Brief Summary

_______Chapter #/ Chapter Title___________________________

Brief Summary

______Chapter #/ Chapter Title_________________________________

Brief Summary

______Chapter #/ Chapter Title_________________________________

Brief Summary

______Chapter #/ Chapter Title_________________________________

Brief Summary

______Chapter #/ Chapter Title_____________________________

Brief Summary

______Chapter #/ Chapter Title_____________________________

Brief Summary

______Chapter #/ Chapter Title_____________________________

Brief Summary

______Chapter #/ Chapter Title______________________________

Brief Summary

______Chapter #/ Chapter Title______________________________

Brief Summary

______Chapter #/ Chapter Title______________________________

Brief Summary

______Chapter #/ Chapter Title______________________________

Brief Summary

______Chapter #/ Chapter Title______________________________

Brief Summary

______Chapter #/ Chapter Title______________________________

Brief Summary

_______Chapter #/ Chapter Title_________________________________

Brief Summary

_______Chapter #/ Chapter Title_________________________________

Brief Summary

_______Chapter #/ Chapter Title_________________________________

Brief Summary

______Chapter #/ Chapter Title__________________________________

Brief Summary

______Chapter #/ Chapter Title__________________________________

Brief Summary

______Chapter #/ Chapter Title__________________________________

Brief Summary

______Chapter #/ Chapter Title_______________________________

Brief Summary

______Chapter #/ Chapter Title_______________________________

Brief Summary

______Chapter #/ Chapter Title_______________________________

Brief Summary

_______Chapter #/ Chapter Title_______________________________

Brief Summary

_______Chapter #/ Chapter Title_______________________________

Brief Summary

_______Chapter #/ Chapter Title_______________________________

Brief Summary

______Chapter #/ Chapter Title_________________________________

Brief Summary

______Chapter #/ Chapter Title_________________________________

Brief Summary

______Chapter #/ Chapter Title_________________________________

Brief Summary

______Chapter #/ Chapter Title________________________________

Brief Summary

______Chapter #/ Chapter Title________________________________

Brief Summary

______Chapter #/ Chapter Title________________________________

Brief Summary

______Chapter #/ Chapter Title_________________________________

Brief Summary

______Chapter #/ Chapter Title_________________________________

Brief Summary

______Chapter #/ Chapter Title_________________________________

Brief Summary

______Chapter #/ Chapter Title______________________________

Brief Summary

______Chapter #/ Chapter Title______________________________

Brief Summary

______Chapter #/ Chapter Title______________________________

Brief Summary

______Chapter #/ Chapter Title________________________________

Brief Summary

______Chapter #/ Chapter Title________________________________

Brief Summary

______Chapter #/ Chapter Title________________________________

Brief Summary

_______Chapter #/ Chapter Title_______________________________

Brief Summary

_______Chapter #/ Chapter Title_______________________________

Brief Summary

_______Chapter #/ Chapter Title_______________________________

Brief Summary

_______Chapter #/ Chapter Title___________________________________

Brief Summary

_______Chapter #/ Chapter Title___________________________________

Brief Summary

_______Chapter #/ Chapter Title___________________________________

Brief Summary

______Chapter #/ Chapter Title____________________________________

Brief Summary

______Chapter #/ Chapter Title____________________________________

Brief Summary

______Chapter #/ Chapter Title____________________________________

Brief Summary

______Chapter #/ Chapter Title___________________________________

Brief Summary

______Chapter #/ Chapter Title___________________________________

Brief Summary

______Chapter #/ Chapter Title___________________________________

Brief Summary

Story
Notes

Section 3:
Revision

The most important thing in life is to stop saying 'I wish' and start saying 'I will.' Consider nothing impossible, then treat possibilities as probabilities.

— Charles Dickens

Revision
Checklist

Before beginning revisions, set the book aside for at least a few weeks so you can come back to it with a fresh perspective.

- Read aloud. Mark where you stumble over the words, then edit for flow.

- Check to make sure the POV is consistent. Does it stay with the main character/s?

- Is the tense consistent throughout the book?

- Are character names consistent throughout the book?

- Spell check. Grammar check.

- Adverbs: Search for words ending in -ly and replace where possible.

- Are there places you are telling where you could be showing?

- Are there places where you are showing, and it doesn't advance the plot?

- Is the voice always true to the character's age?

- Have you written sensory details that use all five senses?

- Is there more than one coincidence moving the plot forward? You shouldn't have more than one per book.

Revision
Notes

Revision
Plot

Use this exercise to write a one or two sentence summary of your novel's plot points. Identify each one.

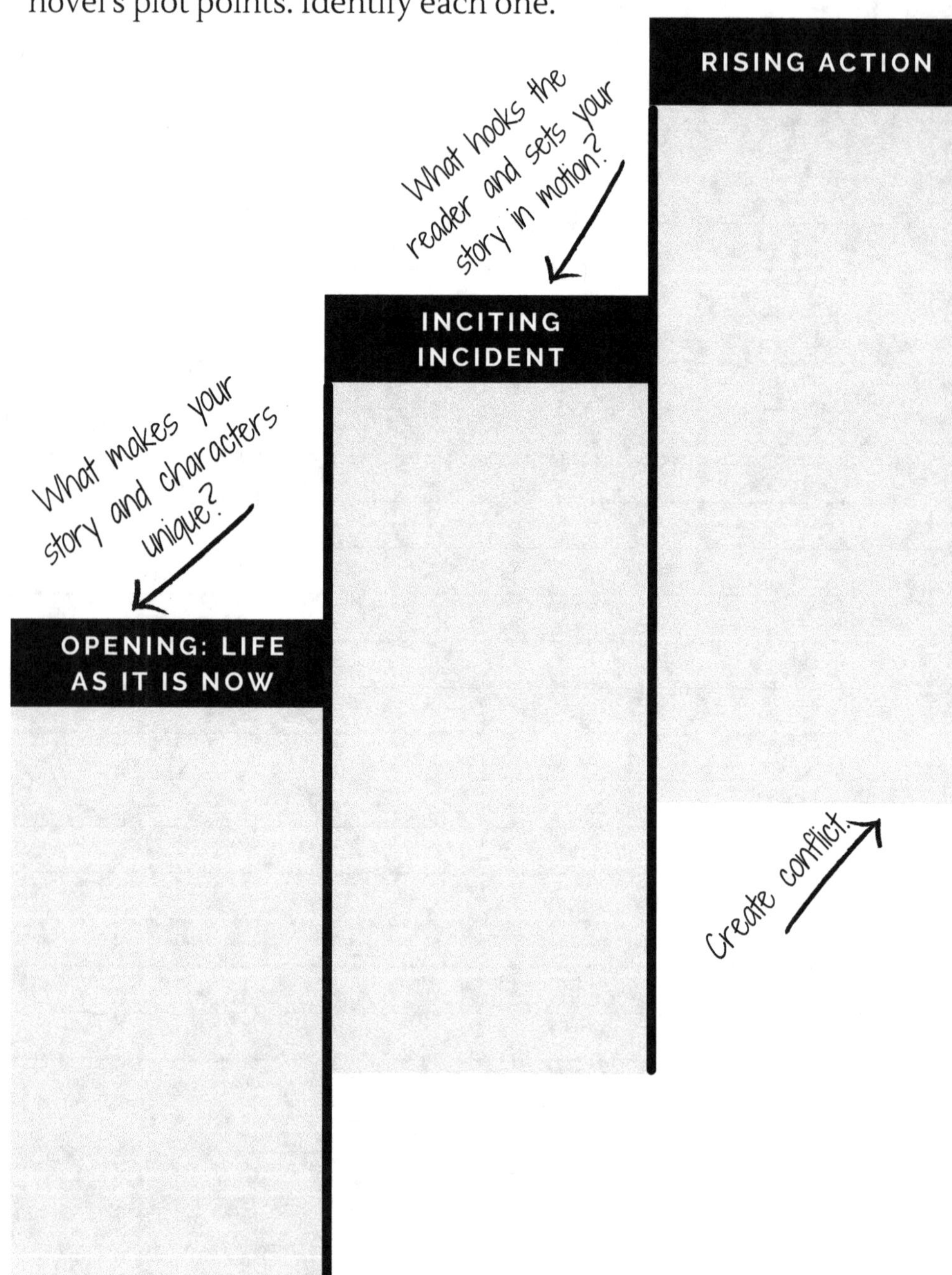

CLIMAX

What is the turning point? ←

FALLING ACTION

What moves your story toward conclusion? ←

RESOLUTION

How does it end? →

Revision Checklist
Pacing

Think about pacing as the speed dial for your story. Where does the action need to move along quickly? Where would slowing down create more effective storytelling? Use this checklist to help you edit for pacing.

- ☐ Chapter length: Does each chapter have a clear beginning, middle, and end?

- ☐ Does the paragraph length vary page by page?

- ☐ Does sentence length reflect the action happening in the story?

- ☐ Do any key details need to be highlighted with more description?

- ☐ Does backstory ever interrupt the flow of the narrative in a distracting way?

Revision
Overused Words

1. Search your document for the following words.
2. See if they can be removed or replaced with something more descriptive and original.
3. Keep a list of words that you tend to overuse and edit if needed.

			MY OVERUSED WORDS
able	great	new	
actually	happy	nice	
amazing	hard	other	
awful	important	quite	
bad	interesting	really	
beautiful	just	sad	
best	like	smart	
big	little	so	
fine	look	that	
first	mad	thing	
funny	many	very	
good	more	well	

Additional thoughts on word choice:
- Rethink any word that's trying too hard to sound cool and modern.

- If you're using slang/current buzz words, make sure they sound original to your writing and true to your characters. Even if your story takes place in the modern world, it is still your version of reality, and your characters don't have to use slang to feel real.

Revision
Avoid Clichés

If you've used any of these in your work, consider changing them to more original language.

- a blessing in disguise
- a dime a dozen
- adding insult to injury
- at the drop of a hat
- beat around the bush
- beat a dead horse
- bite the bullet
- best of both worlds
- bite off more than you can chew
- by the skin of your teeth
- caught between a rock and a hard place
- costs an arm and a leg
- cut corners
- devil's advocate
- don't judge a book by its cover
- don't count your chickens before they hatch
- feel under the weather
- fit as a fiddle
- get a taste of your own medicine
- get a second wind
- give someone the cold shoulder
- go on a wild goose chase
- heard it through the grapevine
- hit the nail on the head
- kill two birds with one stone
- let someone off the hook
- let the cat out of the bag
- like two peas in a pod
- no pain, no gain
- on the ball
- once in a blue moon
- piece of cake
- pull someone's leg
- speak of the devil
- steal someone's thunder
- straight from the horse's mouth
- the last straw
- the elephant in the room
- throw caution to the wind
- your guess is as good as mine

*modern clichés to think about changing in your work:
- living your best life
- you do you
- strong, independent woman
- sorry, not sorry

more on clichés

Maybe you've read something like this recently:

- She clenched her fists so tight that her nails made half-moon indentations across her palm.

Or something like this:

- They didn't realize how hard they were biting their lip until they tasted blood.

These are phrases that aren't exact quotes from books but ones we've read an iteration of so many times they are almost clichés.

As you're editing, look beyond clichés to the actions your characters are taking and make sure they feel original and authentic and yours. Strong voice comes from original use of language. Perhaps your character would bite their lip so hard they'd taste blood. Great. Make the lip-biting original and unique to that specific character, and it won't seem cliché.

Exercise: Choose one of your characters and rewrite the cliché phrases above to sound unique and original to your work.

Fist clench:

Lip biting:

Beta
Readers

Once you've revised your completed draft, you need readers. Choose people who will be objective and give you honest and helpful feedback. These could be other writers, avid readers, or members of your critique group.

Keep track of who you sent it to so you can follow-up and add them to your acknowledgements, if you desire.

Reader	Sent	Returned	Draft# & Take Away

Reader	Sent	Returned	Draft# & Take Away

Revision
Notes

Section 4:
Publishing & Marketing

I declare after all there is not enjoyment like reading! How much sooner one tires of anything than of a book!

— Jane Austen, *Pride and Prejudice*

Finding Good
Comp Titles

Comparison or "comp" titles are important in querying, acquisition, and choosing categories in online stores. These comparisons can often be found on the back of books. For example, "If you're a fan of x then you'll love y."

What Makes a Good Comp Title?

1. How long ago was the title published? Usually comp titles need to have been published within the last five years, or you can mix a classic title with a modern one.
2. Find comp titles that have similar readership. For example, mystery titles for your mystery novel, young adult titles for your young adult novel, and historical romance titles for your historical romance novel.
3. Don't pick books by breakout stars like J.K. Rowling, Stephenie Meyer, or James Patterson.
4. While you don't want to pick an outlier, it's important that the book has had some success. Others need to know and appreciate the comp title.

How Do I Find Comp Titles?

1. Look at the categories on Amazon.
2. On Goodreads or other retail websites, look under the "People who enjoyed this..." section.
3. Ask around. Ask librarians, book sellers, writers, and avid readers. They're all great resources.

Print book covers of comp titles and adhere them to the following pages to help you see the similaries.

Finding Good
Comp Titles

Name: _______________________________________

Why this is a comp title:

____

____

Name: _______________________________________

Why this is a comp title:

____

____

Name: _______________________________________

Why this is a comp title:

____

____

Name: _______________________________________

Why this is a comp title:

____

____

Name: ____

Why this is a comp title:

____

____

Name: ____

Why this is a comp title:

____

____

Name: ____

Why this is a comp title:

____

____

Name: ____

Why this is a comp title:

____

____

Name: ____

Why this is a comp title:

____

____

Write the Perfect
Pitch

A pitch is a concise and interesting description of your manuscript. It needs to be compelling so that it entices others to read your novel.

- What's your manuscript's genre?

- What's your manuscript's word count?

- Who is your main character (MC)?

- What is your MC's goal?

- What prevents the MC from reaching said goal?

- What changes for the MC?

- What's the price of failure? Or the payoff?

Put It Together

My manuscript, (Title), is a (Genre) with (# of words) words. (Main Character) wants to (Goal). But can't because (Obstacle). If he/she can't overcome then (Price of Failure). But if the goal is achieved, he/she will (Payoff). It's (comp title) meets (comp title).

Put It Together

My manuscript, (Title), is a (Genre) with (# of words) words. (Main Character) wants to (Goal). But can't because (Obstacle). If he/she can't overcome then (Price of Failure). But if the goal is achieved, he/she will (Payoff). It's (comp title) meets (comp title).

Put It Together

My manuscript, (Title), is a (Genre) with (# of words) words. (Main Character) wants to (Goal). But can't because (Obstacle). If he/she can't overcome then (Price of Failure). But if the goal is achieved, he/she will (Payoff). It's (comp title) meets (comp title).

Nailing the
Query

Query letters are the first step in getting an editor or agent. They serve as an author's introduction and a way to entice agents and editors to want to learn more about your work. Your query needs to be compelling and concise.

Quick Query Letter Tips:

General Information:
- Queries should convey the voice of your story, but they should not be gimmicky.
- Remember this is a professional letter. Ensure that your formatting, font, and coloring all look the best that you can make it.
- Check individual agent/editor website and follow their submission guidelines.

Format Information:
- No longer than one page
- 12 point font
- Times New Roman
- Single-spaced

Now Let's Get Started

Like all professional letters, begin with a personal greeting. There should not be a "Dear Sir," in your query letter. Address each query letter to the individual agent or editor. Also, make sure to spell their name correctly.

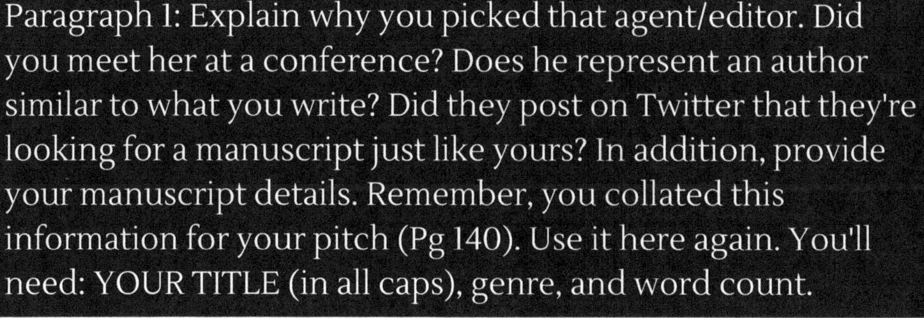

Paragraph 2: Sell your manuscript. Hook the agent or editor with the protagonist, plot, and conflict in your novel. Think about your pitch and expand upon it. (200-300 words)

Paragraph 3: An author biography. This is where you sell yourself. Have you been published? Do you have a degree in writing? Have you won writing awards? Are you a member of a major writing organization or attended a prestigious conference? Is there something in your past or present that makes you the person to write this novel? Do you have a major social media platform? (About 100 words)

Close the query professionally. Thank the agent or editor for their time and opportunity. In addition, include your contact information.

Query Draft

Dear __________________,

____

____

____

____

____

____

____

____

____

____

Sincerely,

Your Name

(Contact Information)

Writing the
Synopsis

The synopsis is a short summary of your story. Now that you've finished and revised your manuscript, it's time to condense it to 1-2 pages. It's not easy but you can do it.

Quick Synopsis Tips:

General Information:
- Needs to be written in 3rd person with a narrative voice.
- Be concise and enticing. You're trying to sell your novel.
- The synopsis needs to include: main characters, plot, conflict, and character arc.
- Reveal the ending. The agents and editors want to know about your complete story.

Format Information:
- 1-2 pages in length
- 12 point font
- Times New Roman
- Single-spaced
- The first time character names are mentioned put them in ALL CAPS.

Synopsis Structure:
- Introduce your story and main character.
- Inciting incident
- Sequence of events relating to the main plot and character arc
- Reveal the end of the story and how the character changed.

All the effort you've put into this workbook is about to pay off. As you fill in the following synopsis questions, refer back to your outlines, chapter summaries, pitch and query sections. You're ready to put this together!

Who are your main characters and what are their goals? Don't forget to talk about your villain.

What is the inciting incident?

What are the obstacles and conflicts in your story?

How does your main character change?

What's the resolution?

Finding the Right
Agent or Editor

Whether you're planning to traditionally publish or self-publish, you'll need to find the right agent or editor. Use this space to record your thoughts on who would be a good fit for you and your project.

Agent/Editor: Agency/House:

Why would they be a great fit?

Agent/Editor: Agency/House:

Why would they be a great fit?

Agent/Editor: Agency/House:

Why would they be a great fit?

Agent/Editor: Agency/House:

Why would they be a great fit?

Agent/Editor: Agency/House:

Why would they be a great fit?

Agent/Editor: Agency/House:

Why would they be a great fit?

Agent/Editor: Agency/House:

Why would they be a great fit?

Agent/Editor: Agency/House:

Why would they be a great fit?

Agent/Editor: Agency/House:

Why would they be a great fit?

Agent/Editor: Agency/House:

Why would they be a great fit?

Agent/Editor: Agency/House:

Why would they be a great fit?

Agent/Editor: Agency/House:

Why would they be a great fit?

Agent/Editor: Agency/House:

Why would they be a great fit?

Agent/Editor: Agency/House:

Why would they be a great fit?

Questions for
Agents

- How long have you been an agent?
- What made you to decide to become an agent?
- Are you a writer?
- How do you communicate with your clients and how often?
- Are you an editorial agent? Will you do rounds of revisions with me on my project?
- How close do you think my manuscript is to being ready for submission?
- What made you connect with my project?
- Where do you see my manuscript fitting in the current marketplace?
- What editors might be interested?

What are some questions that you can add, particular to your writing journey or project?

____
____
____
____
____
____
____
____
____
____
____

Finding the Right
Freelance Editor

Whether you're looking to self-publish or want a professional opinion on your manuscript, you might want to hire a freelance editor.

Freelance editors offer a variety of services; make sure you find the right one for you.

DEVELOPMENTAL EDITS
Editors will cover higher level concepts like plot, character development, voice, emotion, setting, and pacing. Generally, a developmental edit includes in-document edits as well as an editorial letter.

LINE EDITS
Editors take a look at your manuscript at the sentence level. They'll look for things like showing not telling, character voice, word choice, internal thoughts, emotions, and action. Generally, it includes in-document edits as well as an editorial letter.

COPY EDITS
Editors will evaluate your manuscript at the sentence level, looking for things like: grammar, spelling, and punctuation. They'll also watch for any consistency issues with names, setting, timelines, and style.

PROOFREADING
Editors will do one pass through your manuscript and check for any typos or layout problems.

Finding the Right
Freelance Editor

What editor might be a good fit for this project?

Editor: Type of Edit:

What do you like about the editor?

Quote: $

Editor: Type of Edit:

What do you like about the editor?

Quote: $

Editor: Type of Edit:

What do you like about the editor?

Quote: $

Editor: Type of Edit:

What do you like about the editor?

Quote: $

Judging Books by Their
Covers

We say, "don't judge a book by its cover". Unfortunately, the reality is, we all do. The cover introduces your potential reader to your novel so it needs to set the right tone. While traditionally published authors don't usually have a say in book covers, it helps to know the market and what appeals to you as a reader. If you're self publishing, this exercise can help you figure out the design for your cover. Look at a popular book-buying website and find the bestselling novels of your genre. What are the commonalities? What speaks to you from these covers?

Print bestselling book covers in your genre and adhere them to the following pages to see what makes them visually appealing.

Title:____

What works in this cover? _____________________

____

____

Title:____

What works in this cover? _____________________

____

____

Title:____

What works in this cover?________________________

____

____

Title:____

What works in this cover?________________________

____

____

Title:____

What works in this cover?________________________

____

____

Title:____

What works in this cover?________________________

____

____

Judging Books by Their
Covers

What book designers might be a good fit for this project?

Designer: Company:

What do you like about their work?

Quote $:

Designer: Company:

What do you like about their work?

Quote $:

Designer: Company:

What do you like about their work?

Quote: $

Designer: Company:

What do you like about their work?

Quote: $

Designer: Company:

What do you like about their work?

                                                   Quote: $

Designer: Company:

What do you like about their work?

                                                   Quote: $

Designer: Company:

What do you like about their work?

                                                   Quote: $

Designer: Company:

What do you like about their work?

                                                   Quote: $

Designer: Company:

What do you like about their work?

                                                   Quote: $

Writing the
Back Cover

Back copy is vital to the sale of your book. After a potential reader is drawn in by your beautifully designed cover, they will flip it over and read all about your novel. This is where you close the deal. Even if you want to traditionally publish, and much of this is out of your hands, this information is useful to work through.

The back cover can include three things: a description of your book, a blurb, and a picture with a little bit about yourself.

Description of Your Book

To write the description, look back at what you worked on for your pitch (Pg 140) and query (Pg 144). What did you use to hook your reader?

HERE ARE A FEW GUIDELINES
- It needs to be short, under 200 words.
- The tone of your novel should be evident in your description.
- The description should be easy to read and engaging.
- Leave the reader wanting more.

HERE ARE THINGS TO CONSIDER INCLUDING
- Set the scene.
- What is the conflict in your book?
- What must your main character overcome?
- What's the hope for your character?

Back Cover
Description of Your Book

Book Blurb

A book blurb is an endorsement by someone well-known in
your genre. Do you know someone who fits that description?
List anyone who might be willing to review your book.

____

____

____

____

____

Author Biography

Many readers want to know more about the author. Here are a
few tips for writing your author bio:
- Your author bio should be in third person.
- Keep it short (under 200 words) and interesting
- Build your credibility by including major achievements.
- Include previous publications, website, and social media.

____

____

____

____

____

Working on
Inside Information

ISBN Number:

Dedication:

Acknowledgements:

Book Information

Notes

Time to Talk
Marketing

Your book is about to debut. Yay! This is the beginning of a new kind of work. Marketing! While it might be tempting to try and do everything, we suggest you pick the marketing strategies that speak most to you.

HERE ARE SOME IDEAS TO CONSIDER
- Preorder campaign
- Cross promotion with other authors
- Contests
- Cover reveal
- Ask for reviews
- Create video content
- Update your social media frequently with new images and content
- Release deleted scenes or content about your characters or setting
- Set up book giveaways
- Participate in blog and social media events
- Participate in signings, author events, and conferences
- Create a book trailer
- Have a launch party
- Create and share book club questions

Let's Make a Plan

What?

Who can help?

When?

What's your plan?

What?

Who can help?

When?

What's your plan?

What?

Who can help?

When?

What's your plan?

Who can help?

When?

What's your plan?

Who can help?

When?

What's your plan?

Who can help?

When?

What's your plan?

What?

Who can help?	When?

What's your plan?

What?

Who can help?	When?

What's your plan?

What?

Who can help?	When?

What's your plan?

Marketing
Notes

Workbook Author
Bios

Erin Mindes enjoys baking bread, being outside, and spending time with her family. She is the author of *The Lifting Balloons*, an Award-Winning Finalist in the 2020 International Book Awards. Her newest picture book, *Babe, the Ballerina Dog*, will be available with Lawley Publishing in the Fall of 2021.

Stephanie Moore is a wife, mother of four, reader, writer, and quite often, a chauffeur. When not behind the wheel, she binges tv shows and movie series with her family. Moore placed in the Utah Original Writing Competition and is active in the writing community. She is represented by Karyn Fischer from BookStop Literary.

Paige Sommer holds an MFA in Writing for Children and Young Adults from the Vermont College of Fine Arts. She writes for children of all ages. She is a content manager, writer and producer at a publishing company.